Shapes and Solids Outdoors

by Sophie Caribacas

Table of Contents

I need to know these words.

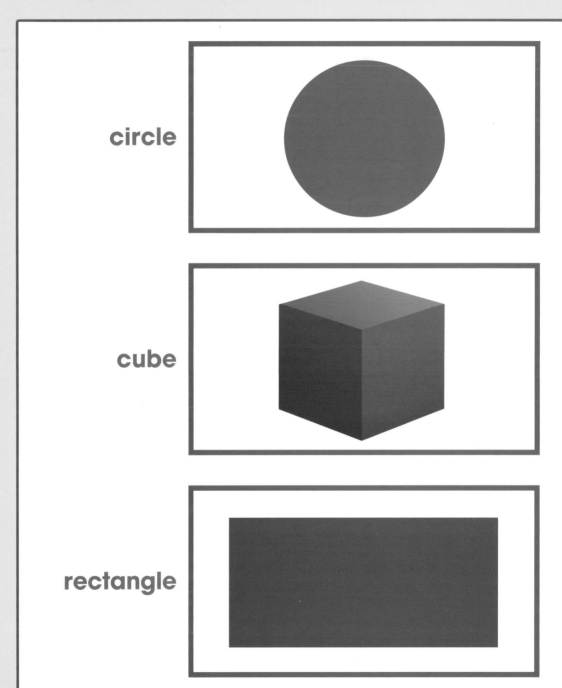

circle

cube

rectangle

rectangular prism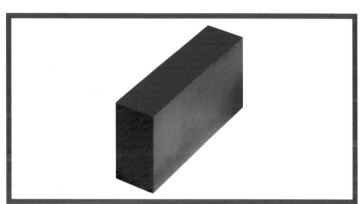

sphere

square

Where Can You Find Cubes and Squares?

Is your home like the home in this picture? This home looks very unusual. This home is a **cube**.

▲ This home is like a big box!

A cube is a solid. A cube has corners and edges. A cube has six faces. The faces are the flat parts of the cube. Each face is the shape of a **square**.

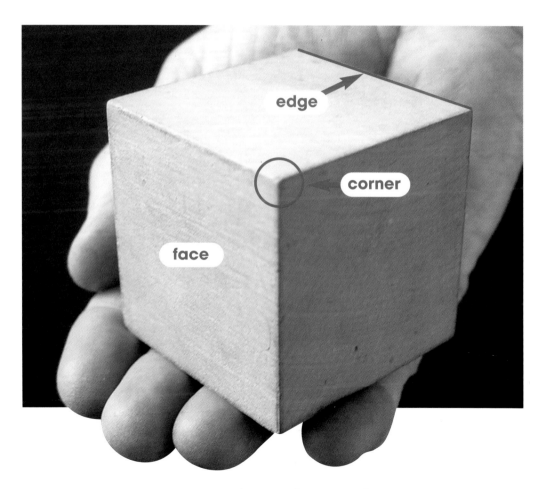

▲ You can see three faces of this cube.

A square is a shape. All shapes are flat. All squares have four sides. Each side is the same length.

square

▲ A square is flat.

Think about squares that you know. You can see squares in games. Can you think of a game with squares?

▲ This game has many squares.

Where Can You Find Prisms and Rectangles?

This building is a **rectangular prism**. How is this prism like a cube? This prism is a solid. This prism has six faces.

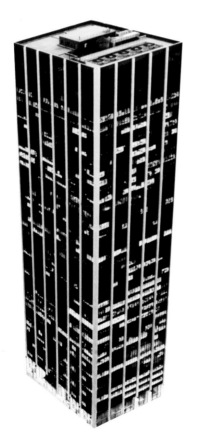 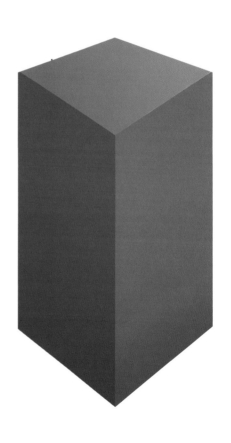

▲ Both of these solids are rectangular prisms.

How is this prism different than a cube? The faces are different shapes. Some faces are squares. Some faces are **rectangles**.

Trace one face of the rectangular prism. What shape did you trace?

face

▲ This box is a prism. This box has faces that are squares and rectangles.

People use prisms every day. People use prisms in many ways. These bricks are rectangular prisms.

▲ This builder uses bricks to make a wall.

You can make a prism from a flat shape. You can fold this flat shape into a box. The box has edges and corners. The box is a prism.

top

flat shape

bottom

top

bottom

▲ The box is a rectangular prism.

All rectangles are flat shapes.
All rectangles have four sides.
This rectangle has two short sides.
This rectangle has two long sides, too.

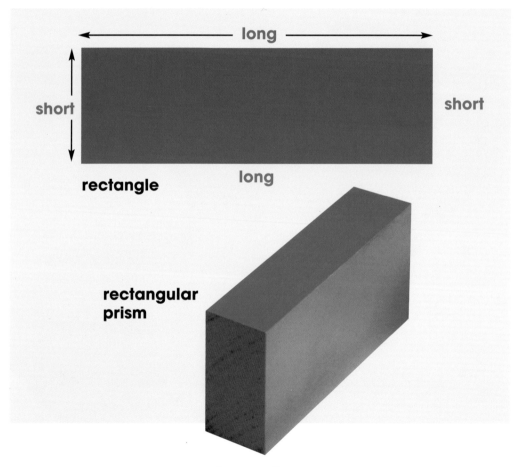

rectangle

rectangular
prism

▲ A rectangle is flat.
A rectangular prism is a solid.

Where do you see rectangles? You can see rectangles in sidewalks. You can see rectangles in art.

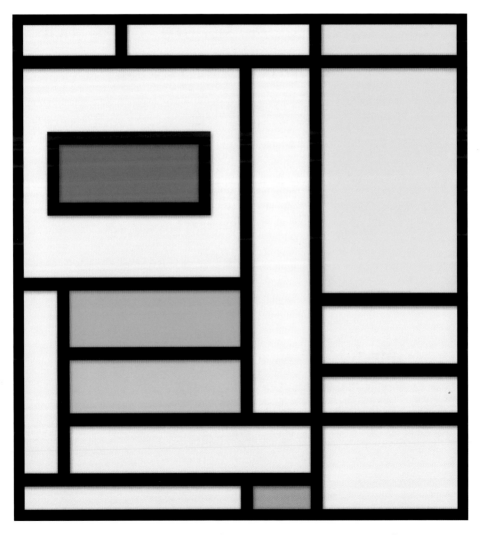

▲ This painting has many rectangles.

Where Can You Find Spheres and Circles?

Some solids are **spheres**. A sphere does not have corners. A sphere does not have faces. A sphere is round.

▲ Earth is a sphere.

A sphere can roll. A ball is a sphere.
People use balls to play games.
The outline of a sphere is a **circle**.

▲ These spheres are different sizes.

A circle is a flat shape. The outline of a circle is curved.

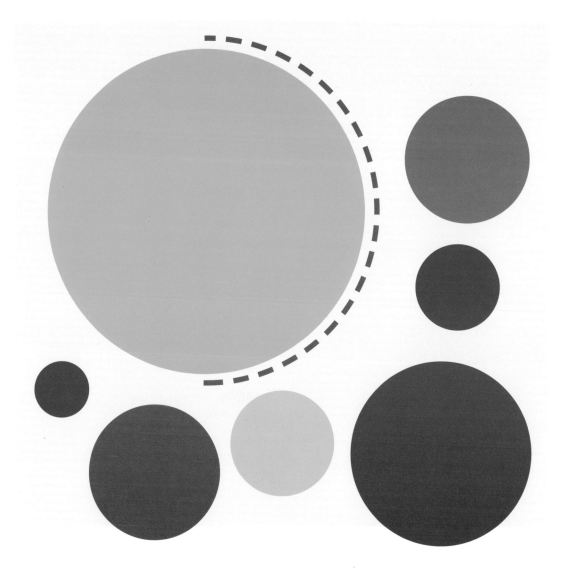

▲ These shapes are all circles.

Look at this cone. The cone is a solid.
Trace a line around the base of
this cone. The outline is a circle.

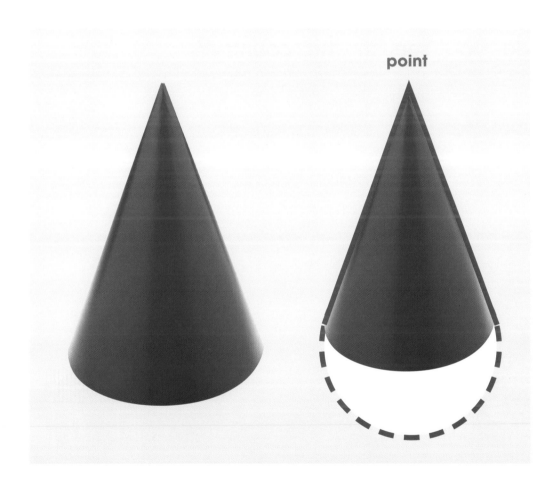

point

▲ A part of the cone is a circle.

Where Can You Find Solids and Shapes?

You can find solids everywhere. You can find solids in the country. What solids do you see in the country?

▲ The buildings are solids.

You can find shapes in the country, too.
What shapes do you see in the country?

▲ What shapes can you see?

Glossary

circle (SER-kul): a curved shape that is flat
See page 15.

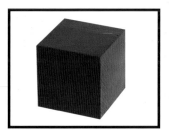

cube (KYOOB): a solid with six faces that are the shape of a square
See page 4.

rectangle (REK-tan-gul): a flat shape with four sides
See page 9.

rectangular prism (rek-TAN-gyuh-ler PRIH-zum): a solid with six faces that are the shape of a rectangle
See page 8.

sphere (SFEER): a solid with no faces or corners
See page 14.

square (SKWAIR): a flat shape with four sides of the same length
See page 5.

Index